Neither Heads nor Tails

Finding the balance
to see the third side
of the coin

by
Anderson Maestri

Church of Christ
Rolla, MO 65401
(573) 364-3488
www.seekgrowservelove.org

ISBN 978-1-893937-43-7 (paperback)

Text Design: Anderson Maestri
Cover Design: Anderson Maestri
Cover Image: Anderson Maestri

© Anderson D. Maestri 2009

All Rights Reserved Under
International and Pan-American Copyright Conventions.
No part of this book may be used or reproduced in any manner
whatsoever without written permission except in the case of brief
quotations embodied in critical articles or reviews.

Printed in the United States by
Independent Publishing Corporation
St. Louis, Missouri 63021

Table of Contents

Acknowledgements	ii
The Allegory	3
The Purpose	11
Section I – Relationships	23
Chapter 1 – Dating	25
Chapter 2 – Marriage	31
Chapter 3 – Parenting	39
Chapter 4 – Friendships	45
Section II – Politics	53
Chapter 5 – School	55
Chapter 6 – Business	63
Chapter 7 – Church	69
Chapter 8 – Government	75
Section III - Personal Choices	85
Chapter 9 – Issues	87
Chapter 10 – Entertainment	97
Chapter 11 – Ethics and Morals	107
The Next Step	117

Acknowledgements

I would like to start by thanking all those who believed in my effort. Those who gave me the extra push to pursue publishing this work. We sometimes understimate the importance of encouraging words and the actions who spark great ideas.

I must also recognize two ladies that were essential in the proofreading of this work. Vanessa and Lisa gave much of their time to assist me. Thank you for your patience and critiques. I really appreciate all the hours we spent going through the chapters.

I am very pleased by the quality service received at the IPC. You guys have smoothed the entire publishing process. And to all those who shared thoughts and ideas that have contributed to the shaping of the final product.

The Allegory

If I was to toss a coin up in the air, what would be my choices? Should I say "heads"... no, maybe "tails"... wait "heads"... ok definitely "tails"! What if, as the coin landed, the outcome was neither... NEITHER HEADS NOR TAILS. What if by some strange chain of events the coin decided not to fall on either side? Normally we would pick it up and toss it up again, but why? Why not accept the third possibility? Why not embrace the third side of the coin?

Both sides seem so definite, so set in stone. "Heads" is always so sure of itself and it will never even look at what Tails has to offer. Tails feels absolutely no need to examine what "Heads" has to say. However, the Third Side looks at both Heads and Tails and realizes that its position is more challenging. It requires more work, and that few tosses will result with the third outcome, but yet it understands that it is exactly where it should remain.

Balanced! Standing between Heads and Tails, unwavering at the attempts to be dragged to either side and tempted to no longer maintain its own personality. By becoming either another Head result or another Tail result, it loses its Third Side peculiarities. Balanced! Standing! It is where the Third Side belongs.

If we consider what makes a coin toss to remain standing, we will find the possibilities that lead the coin to remain on its ideal side. Three options come to mind. By now you are probably wondering what all of this means; the explanation will come after the three options are presented.

• First option: The coin is glued to the surface; it will never fall on either side because the "tosser" didn't really toss it. In this case the coin has no say on the matter, and it will never have any say on the matter because of its circumstances. The coin is completely at the mercy of the "tosser".

• Second option: The coin is held on its end. The "powers to be" keep their finger on top of the coin, keeping it from choosing sides. This option has the coin trapped. The "tosser" gave the coin not even the sense of freedom. It has pressed down any chance or yet impression of freedom.

• Third option: The coin goes into a spin which keeps it from falling on either side. The spin can be caused by simple chance as physics take over and the speed, angle, and trajectory combine to cause the spinning effect as the coin hits the surface. In this case the "tosser" assisted the initial motion, but the coin now is on its own. If it ever stops spinning it will end up becoming either Heads or Tails.

You may still be trying to figure out where I am going with this… Let me share it with you!

The Coin represents us, human beings, creatures with the ability to make rational choices. Choices that require a thought process, a thought process that incorporates instincts, emotions, logic and an evaluation of possible outcomes. We must admit that no animal in this world is so complex when it comes to the business of making choices. An animal has one goal and only one goal, and that is "What keeps me alive?" The animal is not concerned about how this will make its owner feel if it has an "accident" on the carpet. It is also not asking itself "What will society think of me if I eat my own puppies?" An animal's choice is determined by instinct, by its goal of remaining alive.

We, on the other hand, have a large gamut of factors to evaluate both consciously and subconsciously which will ultimately determine our selection. Therefore, as coins, we are being tossed up in the air by the circumstances in our lives. Different forces are pulling us in different directions and trying to influence the final outcome of our decision. The only difference between a real coin and us is the fact that the coin has no real control of the outcome, but WE DO.

The "Tosser" represents the forces to be. It is any event, person, accident, incident, catastrophe, trauma, experience, feeling, lesson, epiphany, or document that pushes us up in the air. Those things that jump start the process of our choices. Those can be millions of moments in life when we come face to face with options. Very few "tossers" have an overwhelming control of the outcome, and usually when they do, our human nature fights it with all fibers of our being because we were created with an innate sense of free will.

Heads and Tails represent the extremes in which we find ourselves when our choices become solidified in one side or the other. As life throws us around and incidents are factored in our choice making equations, we normally find ourselves having to land Heads or Tails. We must be "left" or "right", Liberal or conservative, introvert or extrovert, loved or hated, one or the other. Somehow we have been presented with two extremities that leave us no option but to fight without understanding, argue without seeing the other side.

The Third Side represents balance. It shows that we can stand our ground in a place where options can be weighed without the antagonism of the "opposite" side. It is the ambition of this work. The Third Side is the option that most of us overlook, that even though the world will tell us we only have two options, we must fight the urge to settle, and we must keep spinning ourselves so that we will be constantly looking at both sides, and making our choices based on an objective analysis of all the data. The Third Side allows us to handle every aspect of our lives without giving into extremes.

Here is an example: The coin is you (as a kid), the "tosser" is your father (as a strict parent), Heads represents the fact that you will be just like him when you become a parent, Tails represents that you will become the complete opposite. The Third side represents you learning from him and becoming a balanced individual with the positives of a disciplined father and the kindness wished for in childhood. Sooner or later you will intentionally or unintentionally land on one of the three options.

The symbolism does not end with these initial possibilities; so many other questions clarify the significance behind the third side of the coin and its cause and maintenance. Let me add just a few thoughts for us to consider before we can proceed to the application of this concept. Why would being glued to the third side not be the best scenario? Or why not be held in the "right" position? Who controls if the coin stops spinning or not? Why not Heads or Tails?

Being glued to a position would not allow us to consider the facts. We would virtually become a third extreme. Being held is a matter of human psychology; consider this, if a person meets the guy/girl of their dreams, but for some odd reason is forced to marry him/her, common sense would affirm that any normal human being would be much more comfortable with that outcome if the choice was theirs. Therefore, being forced to pick the "right" side doesn't seem right!

The spinning state is essential for the Third Side. Our desire to maintain a balanced position where we can consider all sides is the main factor that keeps the coin spinning. As long as we want to keep spinning we will keep spinning, and that will keep us on the Third Side. We could get comfortable with an extreme or the other and even without noticing stop spinning.

Heads or Tails are not good choices because they are extremes. There is a difference between being passionate about a position and being blinded to common sense by

biases. My aunt once "yelled" at me when I was a kid. For some reason I was being annoying and insisting in doing whatever it was I wanted to do. I remember her words as if it was yesterday. They made me so mad, but as I grew older they made so much sense. She simply said, "Anything in excess overflows!" That was an interesting way to say "That's enough!" She probably did not realize the depth of her statement. The concept that there is such a thing as too much of a good thing was right then being planted in my mind, so that it could mature for the next twenty years. As a result we come to this assessment, too much to the left we have Tails... too much to the right we have Heads; what option leaves us with just enough?

"Everyone is entitled
to their opinion,
but not everyone is correct!"

The Purpose

As we put two and two together, we must come to realize that ignoring such a concept would cause us to miss out on the wisdom that is in our hands for the taking. Consequently we must see the purpose for such a notion. I would like to present the idea that the Third Side model can be applied in virtually any area of our lives.

Hence this book will enclose a succinct approach to several components of this society we live in. We will be scrutinizing how this conjecture fairs against the background of relationships, or when faced with politics, even input it in the religious equation, or when we blend it with our personal consciousness. I dare to take you on a journey which may change your perception on stubbornness, which may modify your political views, maybe even revolutionize your opinion of self.

Consequently you may ask yourself, "What's in it for me?" What would be the personal reason someone may have that could cause them to spend time in these pages? Simple! This principle is so applicable to anyone and any situation, that you would be letting go, missing out, losing something that is already yours. The knowledge in these pages isn't a new secret. It is mostly what we all already have inside. The points may make you hit yourself and say, "I could have thought of that on my own." But you didn't! All the riches of common sense logic are present in our everyday affairs, but we fail to apply such straightforward concepts to ourselves.

You probably still want to know, "What's in it for you?" I'll grant it to you bluntly: balance. Balance in a world of extremes; clarity to analyze the tough choices in life; flexibility to be able to change an opinion when proven wrong; kind reaction to opposing views; open-mindedness to subjects before disregarded; and finally, you will gain a new perspective on topics you may have overlooked in the past. You can even pick and choose what chapters to spend time on since the chapters are independent of each other.

Hopefully, by now, we are ready to embark in an excursion of the Third Sides that have been long lost in the middle of the battle of extremes. We are ready to start judging for ourselves if the Third Side is actually present in all the areas we are about to engage in.

Too Much of a Good Thing

Before we can start our contemplation of the extremes, we must first do away with the thought that there isn't such a thing as "too much of a good thing". We can find that the Oxford Dictionary of Quotations has dated this proverbial phrase at the late 15th century (Martin, n.d., p.1). This phrase carried the meaning that excess can do you harm; even if it is from a good thing.

We are all very familiar with the "magical" benefits of drinking water, taking our vitamins, even soaking in some sunlight. Society has been bombarded by advices about how much water to drink, what type of vitamins to take, and many other health tips that are actually correct. Thus here is where we start our demonstration that we can, in fact, have too much of a good thing, which would in turn solidify our presupposition that we can find two extremes for any situation.

Let's start this section of our conjecture dealing with drinking water. All of us could scream out a number if asked, "How many glasses of water should we drink per day?" Even doctors have different numbers, but we would all agree that there are undisputable benefits derived from proper hydration. In other words, "water is good for us."

Since our point is to prove that there can be too much of a good thing, let's turn our attention to 28 year old Jennifer Strange, a California wife and mother of three children who died after drinking approximately 2 gallons of water for a radio contest. I cannot fathom the pain of that family, and I feel deeply sorry, but who, before that day, would have thought that water (drinking, not drowning), such a health icon of athletes and health nuts, would be the cause of her death? Maybe a single event is not enough to firm our position down. Allow me to borrow an excerpt from Dr. Ben Kim out of his website drbenkim.com

"Whenever you disregard your sense of thirst and strive to ingest several glasses of water a day just because you have been told that doing so is good for your health, you actually put unnecessary strain on your body in two major ways:
1. Ingesting more water than you need can increase your total blood volume. And since your blood volume exists within a closed system - your blood circulatory system - needlessly increasing your blood volume on a regular basis puts unnecessary burden on your heart and blood vessels.
2. Your kidneys must work overtime to

filter excess water out of your blood circulatory system. Your kidneys are not the equivalent of a pair of plumbing pipes whereby the more water you flush through your kidneys, the cleaner they become; rather, the filtration system that exists in your kidneys is composed in part by a series of specialized capillary beds called glomeruli. Your glomeruli can get damaged by unnecessary wear and tear over time, and drowning your system with large amounts of water is one of many potential causes of said damage."

We can agree that water is a good thing, but we can also agree that drinking too much water can stop being a good thing and quickly become a tragic thing. How about vitamins? There are numerous diseases directly related to the lack of vitamins in our system. I, myself, remember as a kid having to take B12 supplements because of certain pains I was experiencing. I wasn't old enough to remember all of my parents and the doctor's conversations. I couldn't even tell you what was wrong with me. The only phrase that stuck in my head was, "He needs a B12 complex!" Try telling that to your toddler, and then write me, telling me his reaction. It should be very similar to mine!

As kids, as parents, as patients, and as doctors, we all have understood to some level the importance of vitamins to a healthy life. How the lack of vitamins make us more susceptible to certain illnesses. How many of us have been told to drink our orange juice because it has vitamin C, and it will help us avoid catching a cold? Therefore we can say that we agree that vitamins are a good thing. Once again, since we are trying to prove something here, let's look at the effects of having too much of a good thing.

The Canadian Medical Association published at the CAMJ in July 3, 2003, an article which states "high doses of some vitamins, especially when taken regularly, can be toxic"(Wooltorton, 2003) When we are little ones, our parents seem to have the strength of Hercules, the speed of Hermes and, most important to this section, the wisdom of Solomon. They apparently know everything there is to know about anything. That means that when they tell us to eat our vegetables, it is because they know that those veggies contain Beta Carotene, ascorbic acid, vitamin D, vitamin B6 and others. Or maybe our parents got their information from someone else. The following table was taken from the CAMJ website, www.cmaj.ca/cgi/content-nw/full/169/1/47/T127 (Any uses or copies of eCMAJ in whole or in part must include a bibliographic citation, including author(s), article title, journal name, year, volume and page numbers, and the URL www.cmaj.ca, and MUST include the copyright notice that appears with each article.) Copyright notice: This website and each article, abstract, figure, table, image or other content of *Canadian Medical Association Journal (CMAJ)* are protected by copyright.

Table 1: Potential toxic effects associated with selected vitamin supplements*

Vitamin+	Common food sources	Recommended intake for adults	Potential toxic effects associated with supplement
Vitamin A (retinol)	Liver, eggs, oily fish, fortified margarine and dairy products	900-1500 µg (3000-5000 IU)	Hepatotoxic effects, visual changes, hair and skin changes, teratogenic effects at intake >10000-15000 IU/d; potential increase risk of hip fracture at intake > 15000 IU/d
Beta carotene (provitamin A)	Yellow and orange fruits and vegetables, green leafy vegetables	Not applicable	Risk o flung cancer among smokers and people with asbesthosis at intake > 33000 IU/d; yellowing of skin, diarrhea and arthralgias
Vitamin C (ascorbic acid)	Citrus fruits, broccoli, kiwi, yams, strawberries, melons	60-90 mg	Diarrhea, gastric upset at intake > 2000mg
Vitamin D	Liver, eggs, oily fish, fortified margarine and dairy products	10-25 µg (400-1000 IU)	Soft-tissue calcification or hypercalcemia at intake > 2000 IU
Vitamin E	Plant oils (soya, corn, olive), nuts, seeds, wheat germ	15-20 mg (22-30 IU)	Nausea, vomiting, diarrhea, possible antiplatelet effects, headache, fatigue and blurred vision at intake > 800 IU/d
Vitamin B6 (pyridoxide)	Poultry, fish, meat, nuts, legumes, whole grains, potatoes	1.3-2 mg	Sensory neuropathy, ataxia if regular intake > 200 mg/d
Vitamin B12 (cyanocobalamin)	Fish, meat, eggs, milk, some algae and seaweed	2.4-6 µg	No upper limit known
Niacin (vitamin B3)	Meat, eggs, milks, flours	14-20 mg	Vasolidation, gastrointestinal upset, hypercalcemia; potential interactions with statins, antihypertnsive drugs; hepatotoxic effects may occur at intake > 3000 mg/d

*Compiled from information in references 1, 2, 3, 7 and 9

(+)Vitamin K, w hich has an anticoagulant effect, is not available in Canadian multivitamin preparations and thus is not included in the table.

Effects with names such as teratogenic, arthralgias, hypercalcemia, vasodilation, soft-tissue calcification, and antiplatelet are enough to convince me that overdosing on vitamins can be a most unwelcomed experience. Maybe more common-name effects would convince most of us that too much of a good thing (in this case vitamins) is definitely harmful; effects such as visual changes, hair or skin changes, diarrhea, nausea, vomiting and fatigue.

How about the opposite end of the spectrum? When someone mentions soaking up the sun, our minds immediately travel to the lectures about skin cancer. As a result of much awareness created about the subject, we know how harmful too much sun can be. Thus in this case we'll classify "too much of a good thing" as staying out of the sun. If our skin never sees the sun again the chances of any harmful effect would be zero, right? Nope, wrong! Psychiatrist Norman E. Rosenthal, M.D. would disagree as he would explain in his work, Winter Blues: Seasonal Affective Disorder - What It Is and How to Overcome It, where he compiles his studies of this condition that is triggered by the lack of exposure to sunlight (Rosenthal, 1998). SAD is highly linked to depressive side effects, and for people suffering with PMS, alcoholism, bulimia nervosa, panic disorder, sleep disorders, and Bi-Polar disorder, they can have their symptoms peak to a greater level.

If you are going to say that there is no such thing as protecting yourself too much from the sun, consider these symptoms of Seasonal Affective Disorder:
- body aches and pains,
- changes in energy level, appetite
- changes in sleep/wake patterns,
- avoidance of social situations,
- reduction in the quality of sleep,
- drop in energy level,
- weight gain,
- irritability,
- inability to complete tasks,
- decreased creativity,
- suicidal thoughts.

Optimistically speaking these symptoms together with the other two scenarios should be sufficient proof to allow us to bury the thought "there isn't such a thing as too much of a good thing". A person can take any situation to an extreme that will eventually become harmful to self, to others, or both. Thus we must accept that "too much of a good thing" is a suitable concept for our inquiries.

Exploring the Extremes, Finding the Third Sides

Now that we are ready to get underway with our study, it seems like an appropriate spot for us to lay down a navigational map for sections and chapters that are about to follow.

The large subdivisions are sections which hold the general area of application. In every section you will find an introduction to how the Third Side concept applies to that specific area.

Inside every section there are chapters with more specific topics. Those topics will be placed under scrutiny as we observe the existence of the extremes. The topics were selected and arranged without any specific order of importance. All topics are valid and independent of each other, making it possible for the reader to follow the chapters in any desired order.

Each chapter will be composed of Heads examples, Tails examples, and a suggested Third Side. Heads and Tails will be proven existent by allegories, logical deductions, scientific methods, scholarly document, articles, or other means by which the information is brought to my attention.

Section I

"How can those who say that there is no absolute truth know that their statement is absolutely true!"

Relationships

What better way to start than relationships? The epitome of extremes is found in relationships. A state where complete opposite sides of the spectrum come together to clash as people try to merge distinct personalities, different genders, diverse goals, and unique backgrounds. We are involved in relationships in every area of our lives.

If we are not dating, we may already be married. If neither, then we definitely have friends, unless you live alone on an island. One way or another we will have to interact with other individuals. For those that are married, you may not only have the marriage relationship to handle, but also the little ones that so commonly come into play.

In the realm of relationships we will find that while dating we had or have to deal with extremes. After we survive dating, we enter into the blissfulness of marriage. For about 50% of those, bliss is quenched by the extremes when many divorcing couples claim irreconcilable differences. "She chose heads; I chose tails. Now we can't agree on a common ground." In the average course of events, marriage leads the way into parenting, and now we would be dealing with extremes that, in the name of "good" parenting, neglect any form of common sense and common courtesy.

For those who did not fit into any of those relationships, think of your friendships and the challenges that may have appeared throughout your life. How did extreme points of view affect those relationships? How about your different personalities? Some of us are lucky enough that without even thinking about it, we fit into friendships where certain extremes compliment each other, or they are easily dismissed, not causing friction in the relationship.

In this unit we will work our way from dating to parenting and from marriage to friendship. We must keep in mind that the extremes presented here are just the tip of the iceberg. These pages should only spark the train of thought that progresses into many other possibilities.

24

Chapter 1

Dating

Even though many adults are either still in or back in the dating scene, it is a reasonable assumption to think that a larger portion of those involved in dating are individuals from their teens to young adults. The range of extremes is more often than not related to a certain level of emotional immaturity, perhaps even psychological issues.

Puppy love vs. Emotional Skepticism

The first extreme is found in what we call "puppy love". It is an extreme where couples have their feelings so entangled by their false impression that absolutely nothing can go wrong in their relationship. As you can imagine, there are numerous complications that such a mentality can generate.

How many of us, looking in retrospect, can say that "puppy love" was a fact in some early relationship? Ok, if you don't want to admit it, we could say that at

25

least we know someone who has. Either way we are all aware of the concept. For those who have suffered of that extreme, it is probably easy to recognize the nuances of such a position. There are many stories of couples that defied the wise advice of family and friends, that made choices in spite of all red flags, and that hurried into marriage based on that "puppy love". For those who haven't themselves made any of those mistakes, we can safely assume they have witnessed others doing so.

Most of us know exactly how it feels, or how frustrating it can be to see that someone is making the biggest mistake of their lives, but "puppy love" has completely blinded them, and they will not heed any warning. It is scary to look back and imagine where our choices would have taken us if the "puppy love" extreme had won us over.

The opposite end can be just as daunting if we consider the missed opportunities that "emotional skepticism" can cause. On this opposite side of the coin, we find those who, for one reason or another, have developed an unrealistic disbelief of relationships.

This extreme causes many individuals to pursue pointless relationships. Without any desire or faith in romantic love, the person suffering "emotional skepticism" will not only pass by desirable opportunities, but also involve others in relationships which would only lead to heartbreak.

It becomes easy to see in this very first scenario that neither heads nor tails are satisfactory choices. We must ask, "Is there another option?" Yes! The third Side of the coin would be balanced in between the two extremes. A person must fight the urge to ignore the red flags (caused by puppy love) and struggle against a pessimistic approach towards romantic relationships (caused by emotional skepticism).

Here are some simple thoughts when it comes to puppy love and emotional skepticism:
- If it seems too good to be true, it probably is!
- If no one is EVER good enough for you, then the problem is probably YOU!

Needy vs. unattached

These extremes can be so detrimental to our chances of finding a significant other, or if we are on the receiving end of it, it can be simply aggravating. My apologies to those who are needy or unattached, but if you choose to remain at either extreme, you are choosing to put yourself or your loved ones in a very unpleasant position.

27

The needy person has ignored the age-long rule of dating — "The needier you are, the less attractive you become." It is similar to the simple rule of supply and demand. The product is "personal availability." As we increase the amount of our "P.A." (supply), demand starts to be satisfied; once demand is met, any extra supply will naturally be ignored, resulting in the lower value assigned to "P.A."

In contrast the unattached person doesn't realize how much he is hurting the other person involved. Sooner or later, the other person will realize the lack of attachment and leave, or what is even worse, remain in a harmful relationship. This side treats others in a manner that makes them feel unappreciated, or insecure in the relationship. As you can deduce, this position does not generate positive outcomes.

The third option seems obvious in this case. We must need them just enough, so they will feel wanted, and must appreciate them so they don't see us as unattached. Thus the right mix of both sides makes for an excellent third option.

Easily committed vs. afraid of commitment

"He got dumped last week, and yesterday he found the new love of his life. But three relationships ago he was so sure she was the one." That seems like something I've heard before. It represents a repeated scenario where a person easily jumps into a committed relationship. The reasons why are a mystery to me, but I know there are plenty of those out there.

This type of behavior can be detrimental both in a superficial level and deeper emotional level. The person who jumps head first into relationship after relationship rarely considers healing time. That could cause every relationship to be just as flawed as the past one. Thinking superficially, one could say that a person can slim down his/her chances of finding a desirable relationship, considering the fact that changing relationships like changing shirts makes a person look less like an attractive candidate.

How appreciated would you feel if that person expressed his/her commitment to you after having expressed that same love for another ten people? But the opposite is not pleasant either. How many people jump from relationship to relationship, not because they easily commit but because they never commit? We would most likely be unappreciated because that person would

29

soon find an excuse to leave us. Here is a way to assess if someone is too far one way or the other; simply gauge the expression "I love you". Some may blurt it out like they would say, "Hi. How are you?" Others would hesitantly or maybe even never say it. There is a certain level of credibility that a person can "sense". Even though we may choose to ignore it, we do know if the "I love you" was too hasty or too overdue.

What is the middle ground? It is like getting in a tub of really hot water. You get your toes wet. They burn, so you back off a little, but then you stick your whole foot in. It is hot and it itches from your skin adjusting to the temperature. Then you sit down. It still burns and itches but you hold it long enough that your body gets used to it. Now you are completely in, and there is no way you are getting out. The towel is so far and there is all that cold air between you and warmth. As you can see, commitment is just like that, you take your time getting in, you test the waters, but once you are in, you are in for good.

Chapter 2
Marriage

In this type of relationship, the stakes are much higher, and extremes can be the cause of a lifelong horrible commitment, or a short-lived marriage. Either option is unacceptable. Maybe if we improve ourselves and how we treat our spouses, we may be able to have more pleasant marriages or even avoid a number of divorces. No, this is not a panacea for marriage problems, but I hope to spark some thoughts.

Overbearing vs. "uncaring"

There are some similarities between an overbearing and a controlling spouse, but the difference is found in the definition of overbearing. The American Heritage Dictionary defines it as "Domineering in manner; arrogant"("Overbearing", 2000, p.1). Although we may not mean to be arrogant or we may not think of ourselves that highly, the manner in which we present our opinions can be very overbearing. Now apply that into our day to day life. Imagine being undermined by

31

your spouse for 10, 15, or 20 years, feeling like you had no room to breath. It is sad to say that it would not be surprising if that marriage didn't end up well.

On the other side of the coin, we find the spouse that couldn't care less if you won the Nobel Prize or if you groomed yourself today. The "uncaring" extreme not only doesn't try to dictate your decisions, it doesn't have any interest in them. It is a depressing reality to think that there are couples who actually display signs, sometimes more than just signs, of such an extreme. Let me ask you to imagine yourself in that situation.

How does it feel to receive a cold "congratulations", if that much, after sharing the news of a personal exhilarating achievement? How does it feel to have someone you want to share everything with, not care about what you have to share? I know for sure it doesn't feel good, and if you say "it's not that bad", you are lying to yourself.

A couple's goal should be to strive to care enough to make your loved one feel appreciated and cared for, but not to the point where we become overbearing. Let them make their decisions, then be there to rejoice with the great results and mourn with the negative ones. Let go of what "I" want, and focus on what is best for "Us".

Too controlling vs. too indecisive

"Where would you like to eat?" she asks. "Any where is fine," he answers. It seems like a normal conversation, but the reality of this routine is that it happens at every instance of their marriage. Deciding what to eat is only the tip of the iceberg. Underneath we will find that the indecisive spouse cannot make a choice on his/her own. It is normal to be indecisive one day or another, in one situation or another, but we are discussing extremes, and this edge can drive a spouse insane.

How encouraging or attractive really is someone who cannot decide anything on their own? Transfer that into a marriage situation. How secure or motivated will a spouse that is too indecisive make us feel? Or if we are the indecisive one, have we considered the stress put upon our spouse? How much easier would a trip be to get some fast food, if the answer was quick and simple? When asked, "What would you like to eat?" without a stutter the answer comes out, "I'm hungry for a burger. How about you?" All of a sudden this simple act became a subconscious demonstration that we know what we want.

If that decisiveness permeates into other areas of our lives, we have become spouses capable of contributing towards a less stressful marriage. We can fulfill one of the top needs in relationships, the sense of security.

Some of us know what we want a little too well. We are so sure of what we want that we extend our desire for that specificity to our spouse in a "not so cordial" way. The spouse who is too controlling makes it clear that things will be done his/her way. The clothes we wear, the friends we have, the jobs we apply for — they are all items which the controlling spouse would determine our choices for us.

It is easy to realize that this extreme is one that can quickly lead to or be a sign of an abusive relationship. If we find ourselves on either end of this bargain, we must immediately focus our efforts in trying to remedy the behavior. If we look in the mirror and see ourselves as a controlling spouse, we should take a step back and put on their shoes. Or if we find ourselves in an abusive relationship, being completely controlled by our significant other, we must seek help.

The balance in this case is: We must improve and know ourselves so that we know what we want from ourselves, from others, and from life. And that would trickle down to the little aspects of our marriages. But if we find ourselves demanding that choices be made

34

constantly our way, and not considering the well-being of our marriages, then we may have gone a little too far towards the controlling side.

Big spender vs. penny pincher

This is a Marriage 101 basics course classic. How many statistics have we heard about marriage problems originating from money issues? If we combine a penny pincher with a big spender, what do we get?

a)   The perfect balance to make a financially stable marriage.

b)   A stressful relationship where someone is not getting their needs fulfilled

c)   A ticking time-bomb waiting to explode in a divorce.

The answer is actually all of the above. There is a chance that any of these results may happen.

The big spender has probably learned from family or environment that we must live for the day, and that the "right" attitude towards money should be "If you have it, then use it." This idea merges well with a certain carelessness about long-term planning. An expression I learned as a child fits very well in this situation: "If I eat cabbage for a while now, I can eat much better in the future." A big spender would not consider the fact that by eating more than cabbage today; he/she may lack even the cabbage tomorrow. The big spender has a poor sense of delayed gratification.

As we flip to the other side, we find the penny pincher. Someone whose fear of spending money is so branded in them that the thought of buying something without extensive consideration is a foreign concept. The expression ignored by the big spender is usually magnified and dogmatized by the penny pincher. He/she may lose sight of the reason for "eating cabbage today". He/she may forget that we do so in order that we may "eat better in the future."

Option A will only be possible if both sides learn to compromise and accept that they have extreme points of view when it comes to spending money. They must work together to find a safe middle ground for their spending habits. If a third side for this coin is not found, then it is heartbreaking to say that we are left with options B and C.

Too much time with family vs. Too little time with family

Half of this topic would seem to go against what most family counselors have been telling couples lately. In a society where "tempus fugit" (time flies), where people wish the day was 28 hours long because we are all so pressed for time, spending or not spending time with our families has become a common source of problems for spouses who are trying to earn a living and maintain a healthy marriage.

The side which most counselors are dealing with is "too little time". Couples work longer hours, or sometimes different shifts, causing them to be away from each other. Few of us are fortunate enough to work close to home where we could enjoy a short break spent with our loved one, like coming home for lunch. Sometimes after a long day at work, our moods are altered and we don't feel like spending time with anyone, and we bury ourselves in whatever activity that would give us that isolation. If such pattern goes unchecked for too long, the end result could be very painful.

However, painful results can also spring from spending "too much time" with our families. Once again, let us turn on our extreme mindset, and picture what "too much time" means. I would guess most of us have heard the expression "breathing room". If we spend enough time with someone without any breathing room, it is virtually certain that tensions will rise and frustrations will thrive in those situations. Consider reality TV. Have you ever noticed that there is never any sort of entertainment which would give them constant breaks from each other? Producers want drama, fights, and bickering to get better ratings, so what do they do? They make sure those people spend "too much time" together.

Our marriage is not immune to this phenomenon. We, as individuals, need time for ourselves. There are plenty of cases where a spouse demands to spend every second of their free time with their other half, and chooses to ignore their need for individuality. That causes a tremendous burden that in short-term can be annoying, but in the long run it can be a marriage killer. Therefore, for the sake of marital health, we must find the balance between too much or too little time spent with our spouses. We can be entangled by either side. And these sides are a little harder to measure, since when we usually notice it, damage is already taking place. Thus I would advise couples to use the third side of the coin as a preventive tool, to strive towards a balance prior to forming any pattern of behavior. For those who find themselves already on one edge or the other, I sympathize with the battles ahead, and pray that you will have the wisdom, patience and strength to fight those battles.

Chapter 3

Parenting

Here we have two sides which will affect a defenseless third party. The subject of child rearing is a touchy one. Parents who are so cool and collected about most things in life can become irrational cavemen who will start swinging their clubs to defend their litter at the first sign of "danger". Emotions take over common sense and walls are put up in the name of "good parenting."

What some parents don't realize is that you don't have to be perfect. In our quest to be the perfect parents, or to ease the guilt for being so busy with our lives, we have created extreme parenting styles that will do more harm than we think. The Boston Globe printed an interesting article entitled "Raising a perfect child" written by Beth Wolfensberger Singer, which I would like to share a segment with you. This portion of the article shows society's trends that swing from one extreme to the other.

39

Strict parenting vs. loose parenting

"Raising a perfect child" By Beth Wolfensberger Singer

During the 1940's and '50s, Braun explains, a common child-raising style was what might now be termed authoritarian*: I'm the parent, you're the child, and I'll tell you what to do because I know better, and you'll do it. "There were societal expectations for how people should behave," she says, "and they were sort of set from the top, and children complied. But a lot of children grew up fearful, or angry, or humiliated, or resentful. And they said, 'I'm not going to do that to my children.'"

In the late '60s and throughout the '70s, with the erosion of blind respect for authority, the civil disobedience movement "slipped into parenting," Braun says, and parents became very understanding and lax*, wanting to let their kids act on their feelings. "So it got to the point where people stand in a coffee shop, and they see these parents saying to their kids, 'So what would you like, the raspberry Danish or the cherry?' And the kid whines, 'Oh ... I don't know ... I don't want anything.' And there's a line of 12 people, and they're all thinking, 'What is the matter with parents today? This is crazy!'"

Many **permissive*** parents realized the craziness of catering to a child's every whim, so they swung back in the authoritarian* direction, studying books with such titles as Because I Said So! and Spoiled Rotten: Today's Kids and How to Change Them. This took place in the late '80s and throughout the '90s, but it wasn't an effective correction, in part because parents still feel guilt about how little time they have with their kids. "Working parents have a really hard time setting limits and boundaries," Braun says sympathetically. "And children need limits and boundaries as much as they need love and understanding." [*Emphasis mine] (Singer, 2000, ¶ 18-20)

During my fifth grade year we had posters at my school which promoted the idea that saying "No" to children was a bad thing. As a fifth grader I was in paradise, but after years in the education field I have come to understand how flawed that philosophy was. The lack of accountability created by the permissive or likewise, the over-protective side has generated an enormous amount of headaches for educators across the country.

In contrast, the strict style pushes a child toward resentment, anger or worse. I admire our military services, but a home is not a miniature boot camp for life. The excessively strict parent does not realize that some of his/her expectations are unrealistic. After all, kids will be kids. All we can do is make sure we hold them accountable for their actions so that they may learn appropriate boundaries. If in our effort to be strict we don't lend a listening ear, we may neglect the need for safety which the child requires.

We are trying to achieve a balanced point, where children know that there will be consequences (preferably consistent ones), but that they are still secure, heard, and cared for in our love. We are reaching for a parenting style that is strict enough to set important boundaries, but loose enough to know when to lighten up. In my years as a high school teacher, I learned from one of my mentors that I should start the school year with a tight grip of my classroom and as the students learned their limits, I could lighten up and still maintain control of the classroom. And my mentor was right. The third side is found in a consistent and age appropriate approach to our parenting styles.

Too much time with family vs. too little time with family

The same principle which couples must consider in their relationship should also be applied to parents and their children. Kids have some of the same tendencies adults have, and will pay the cost of spending too much time with their family or spending too little time with them.

In the case of spending "too much time", we find that issues ranging from high levels of dependency and separation anxieties to lack of appreciation for the family and increased rebellion are present in those relationships. Like any individual, children need time to figure things out on their own. Sometimes a scratch teaches us more as kids when our parents are not around.

During my kindergarten year, I learned that I reacted differently to pain whether or not my parents were around. It was recess time and I was away from the group playing by myself, climbing on the playground equipment. As I was monkeying around, I turned upside down hanging by 8 fingers (opposable thumbs weren't a factor that day), which started slipping. I knew what was about to happen, so I braced for impact. A head-first collision with the gravel below would have been enough to make a grown man cry, but neither mom nor dad were around. That little detail changed my immediate reaction; I discovered that I was able to handle the pain. So I rubbed it better and went back to class.

Overprotective parents cause their kids to feel overwhelmed because of too much time sheltered under their wing. But if we flip too far to the other side, we could find ourselves spending too little time with our kids.

Spending too little time with our children can cause an abundance of psychological issues for children to battle as they grow older. One of any child's needs is the need to feel loved, and when parents have their children spending the majority of the day with a daycare provider, they have a hard time recognizing that as being loved. As adults we develop love languages that could translate working long hours as "I love you, so I work hard for you". However, children most likely don't have that interpreting power. This type of environment facilitates the development of defiant and/or delinquent behavior. Lack of appropriate time spent with our children generates inadequate attention, insufficient discipline and scarce moral teaching.

Modern day society has added new challenges to raising a family. It is our goal to find the adequate balance, and work towards decent time management skills, so that we can spend enough time with our kids without overwhelming and stifling their individuality. That is the third side which we should strive for in this case.

Chapter 4

Friendships

Not as binding as dating, spouses or children, friendships are often considered dismissible when the two sides of the coin conflict to an unbearable point. Many people don't realize that even friendships are a type of relationship that requires attention and care. It is easy to test that thought. Simply consider your high school friendships. How many of those "best" friends are still around? One? Maybe two? How about those friends that you thought would be friends forever, but now are just good memories at reunions? Any friendship that is uncared for will inevitably wither and at least become healthy nostalgia. Therefore recognizing the two sides in our friendships may assist us in maintaining healthy ones.

Needy vs. "uncaring"

Similar to a needy dating relationship, a needy friend can also require an absurd amount of attention. If you haven't had a needy friend, allow me to paint a picture: Constant phone calls, invitations for every single activity, sharing absolutely everything, and other requirements that when poorly met would result in pouting, hurt feelings and childish distancing behavior. A needy friend can quickly become a burden that some wouldn't hesitate detaching themselves from. Not many people have enough patience to look through the demands of a needy friend.

The other extreme can be just as unhealthy, but with different personal side effects. An "uncaring" friend tends to have a more self-centered outlook on friendships. The focus of such relationship lies on what a person can gain from being associated with others. There is very little to no consideration for what is best for the other person or the relationship in general. We can understand how damaging such a friendship can be.

The equilibrium in this case derives from us being self-secure and yet considerate of the ones around us; appreciating the need for meaningful friendships and striving for a deeper concern for something other than "what's in it for me?" Friendships can be very profitable emotionally, spiritually and sometimes even materially, but if we approach it in an unbalanced way, it could be short lived.

Bossy vs. pushover

My best friend in high school was distancing himself, and I was confused as to why such a thing was happening. We were "best buds", yet he didn't seem to be very happy with our friendship. Finally it was brought to my attention that without noticing, I was very bossy. I would push him around and not realize how hurtful my demanding behavior was.

A bossy friend can build relationships that are as fragile as crystal or as superficial as a teenage boy's outlook on beauty. Most bossy people are not fully aware of how severe their dominant behavior can be. Infringing on a person's boundaries is not the way to build long-lasting bonds. Resentment and distancing oneself, among other things, are common reactions to a bossy friend. In a worst case scenario we can find a warped symbiotic relationship between a needy friend and a bossy friend, like a shark and a remora. Unlike in the animal world, a human friendship cannot survive in such conditions.

A pushover friend exemplifies the other side of the fence. People who can't say no, creatures of "Yes Ma'am/Yes Sir" behavior compose this category. Some do it without noticing. Others know what they are doing but wrongly perceive that they must act this way in order to be accepted. This type of behavior tends to enable the bossy friend's behavior, for the lack of confrontation strengthens the bossy one's sense of entitlement to such conduct. Therefore by being a pushover, we would be doing ourselves twice the disservice.

In my case, a friendly confrontation was all it took for me to desire altering my behavior. A third party brought what was happening to my attention, and it was up to me to get over my pride and reevaluate how I expressed myself.

Section I
Quick Review

In relationships, heads and tails will certainly affect all those involved. Some individuals may profit from the extremes. However our goal is to do the best we can so that everyone involved comes out benefiting from every relationship. Therefore, we must strive to find the third side of the coin. Balance would bring the desired outcome whether we are dating, married, raising children, or even dealing with friendships.

"If the grass is greener on the other side of the fence, you should probably start watering yours!"

Section II

**"Change is not impossible,
it is undesirable!"**

Politics

In this area, extremes are harder to measure but they have more impact in every turn (i.e. moral, social and economical) society takes. We tend to automatically think of government when we hear the word politics, but politics are present in many other areas of our lives.

One of the definitions for politics in the Cambridge Advanced Learner's Dictionary is "the relationships within a group or organization which allow particular people to have power over others" (2008). Politics are a part of any group in which decisions must be made, and those decisions direct the course taken.

We will find politics in schools, businesses, churches, and of course, government. All those areas require decision making to happen, and when decisions need to be made, feelings, ethics, morals, opinions, the end result, among others — all must be considered. The process of evaluating all those and managing to persuade people that this is the course we should take is what we call "politics".

"Without accountability, chaos is emminent!"

Chapter 5

School

In the school realm, politics are present from the administration to the student body to the individual. Every level of interaction has the common characteristic of having someone desiring to lead the "group" towards the "ideal" path.

The administration in its task of creating an environment that is conducive to student development must keep in mind that even though their decisions seem perfect in their own eyes, there are parents, students and even the government which must be convinced of the course taken.

Ideally, students should only have to worry about learning and getting good grades, but the reality is different. Anyone that has been through the school system can agree that we all must deal with fitting in or not, friends and "cliques"; even school spirit or the lack thereof affects our personal connections.

Therefore what is taught, how we act, advocating our ideas, and many other actions in school will involve politics, where one group or another, or one person or another will have an ultimate say in the direction in which we will be led.

Liberal vs. conservative

School districts each have their own specific clientele to cater to. As decisions are made, administrators, principals, and superintendents must consider politics on multiple levels. Every school will have a variety of parents to please. That causes extremes to be a sure way to generate turmoil within the community.

A liberal approach to education and how our children are being brought up while we are at work can be a touchy subject. Some progressive ideas, of what our children should or should not be exposed to, are simply scary. Let me try to illustrate this point. Imagine a school is advocating an earlier age for kids to be exposed to sexual concepts, and that same agenda promotes a sheltering of our children's self-esteem. As a parent, how do you feel about this scenario? Better yet, how would you like your child to be taught that there are no "losers" only "winners"? Or if it is ingrained in them the idea of change for the sake of change and not for a purpose?

How will a principal sell his/her philosophies to a community? If he/she has a liberal agenda, it may be hard to convince the conservative parents and government officials involved, which begs the same question to the opposite side. How would a conservative administrator sell his/her ideas to a crowd that wants, or even needs, a fresh approach?

A conservative leader may not be as receptive to new ideas that could benefit the student body. Think back if you can remember, or imagine if you were not there, a time when there was one type of instruction, and if you didn't get it, tough luck. During all the years I was involved in education, I quickly learned that children learn in different ways. I considered myself a conservative, an "old fashioned schooling got me where I am today, so it should also work for children today" kind of guy. I was in for a rude awakening when dealing with auditory, visual, kinesthetic and tactile learners. If you add all the personal issues that society has created for these children, then we have a recipe for disaster if we don't adapt to their needs.

The solution would consider both sides of the coin, and create a balanced course of action with logical choices that either side could not ignored. And favoring would not be for one extreme or the other, but it would actually be towards the intellectual and emotional well-being of our children.

Do all to fit in vs. do all to stick out

In the student side of this issue, we find those who will do anything to fit in and blend in with certain groups, and others who will purposely stick out. Both extremes are in fact a political struggle of those trying to be heard.

The ones who will do anything to fit in want to be heard by their peers; therefore they will change how they look, how they talk, and who they associate with. This side of the coin can be extremely stressful for those doing all the changing. We could compare it to a politician who is trying to gain the votes of one electorate without losing the votes of the other group. If a kid can accomplish that in school, he/she is a successful "politician". Those will be able to control power-determining trends and fashion statements that will define (divide) the dreaded school cliques.

On the other side of the coin we find the ones who will exert power by standing out, and make statements by being different. These handle the school politics with an "I don't care what you think" frame of mind. Some even dare to break some rules just to be noticed. All of that is a simple struggle to be heard, to feel like our opinions matter, and that someone cares what we have to say.

I suggest that our lives would be much easier if we can have a third option. A choice where we are not sell outs, but we are not rubbing against the grain either. We must strive to create an environment where we can fit in without losing our individuality. A place where we can be different and yet accepted. But that will only be possible if students who do have the power to guide the "mob", would choose to influence the student body to be a "neither heads nor tails" type of group.

Excessive determination vs. apathy

Students and teachers alike all have to deal with this aspect of school politics. As we apply ourselves to our responsibilities, we could end up falling on either side of the fence. This is an area where keeping a balanced approach to our dedication can be fairly easy.

Although we can effortlessly remain balanced, it is also not hard to find those who have fallen towards either side of this coin. Those obsessed with their studies tend to overlook the fact that when employers or colleges are reviewing our resumes, they want more than straight A's. Yes, they want straight A's, but they also seek for someone who is well-balanced socially, and the extracurricular activities demonstrate different levels of social involvement that make those opportunities flourish. This is a political struggle for those trying to exercise power over the outcome of their future endeavors.

On the flip side, we find those who lose any capability of influencing their future opportunities. They are those who have become apathetic to their studies, their school activities, those who somehow are going through their "midlife crisis" during their school year. I question that it would be a real midlife crisis, but let's give them the benefit of the doubt. That apathy can be caused by real psychological conditions or by adolescent drama. Some don't leave that stage until their 30s. Others never leave. Whatever reason may have caused the apathy, I dare say maybe even laziness, the outcome is what worries me. Little to no scholarships for college, fewer acceptance letters from college, lack of job opportunities in a competitive market, these are only a few of all possible consequences for someone who gave up his power to control the course.

As we place both sides face to face, we can see that a third side must be present; otherwise we will have a very depressing outlook on our potentials. Yes, we must strive for straight A's so that we can have some control of our future choices, and yes, we should every now and then let go of certain things so that we can enjoy the journey as much as the end result. So I declare: Be determined but not obsessive; be laid-back but not apathetic! The politics within ourselves is to have the power to control our choices, but also the freedom to enjoy those choices.

"Just because the solution
is simple, do not think
it is easy or desireable!"

Chapter 6

Business

I learned working with my father in our family-owned billboard company, that in the field of business politics, your relationships can be more valuable than money. Exercising influence with clients, competitors, and the authorities through healthy relationships is priceless.

I believe my father was able to accomplish that so well because of his well-balanced approach to dealing with all three groups of people. The magic takes place when deals, transactions, agreements and other operations are slightly swayed by the sense of respect and trust that those relationships can generate.

Take, for instance, being chosen by a client because of the good rapport despite the higher price. In a different case, good business politics prevented major companies from swallowing the little fish, even though taking over would have eliminated some competition. Good business politics will open opportunities and generate a profitable environment to all those involved.

Bossy vs. push-over

Just like in friendships, when dealing with business affairs, a person must know when to stand their ground and when to be flexible. This would require a dedicated attention to the third side of this coin. One might gravitate towards a bossy, unwavering position while others may feel compelled to remain at the comfortable push-over side.

Let's pretend that we will decide how to approach our businesses with the flip of a coin. If it lands "heads," we will be bossy; if it lands "tails," we will be a pushover. First flip takes place and it lands "heads."

A bossy attitude towards business politics can produce resentment, enemies, undesired attention, bad rapport, unhappy employees and clients, and unstable partnerships. Some people are so determined in getting their way that they forget that when it comes to commerce we must consider more than just the immediate results. The extra buck we make today may be the cause of 100 dollars lost tomorrow.

Now we flip the coin again, and it lands "tails." A pushover attitude will create a sense of unreliability and distrust. Competitors will move in like sharks smelling blood, clients will lack confidence in our service, and employees will lack the fear or respect necessary to perform at ideal standards. When people have the impression that we will be easily pushed around, we completely lose the ability to exercise control of any situation. We leave ourselves at the mercy of our competitors, clients and employees.

The challenge then falls into the task of influencing the most results so that the most profit can be made with the greatest amount of satisfaction from all parties concerned. That can only be accomplished through proper balancing of flexibility and firmness, which would be neither heads nor tails, but a third option combining the qualities of both extremes and discarding the flaws.

Big spender vs. penny pincher

Picture a company that is being started from scratch: starting from the idea, buying the first supplies, having two partners and a little capital. Now imagine this same company a month later with two secretaries, one intern, and several employees. Add to the equation the fact that the company didn't grow miraculously, and its revenue is consistent with that of a one-month-old company which started from scratch. You see where I am going with this.

The big spender squanders the company's capital in elements that are many times cosmetic. Some have fully adopted the philosophy that we must look the part in order to become it, so we can witness spending decisions that are an effort to appear big, when in fact the company can barely pay its employees. These people will have to use great politics if the money they are trying to "waste" is not theirs. That is usually when board meetings can turn into heated arguments over budget and spending, especially if the penny pincher is present.

At the risk of swinging too far the penny pincher way is where the sacrifices would be made. Quality control becomes secondary to money saving. Fairness towards workers' wages and benefits becomes an obstacle. Cutting corners and sloppy work could appear as common traits of the penny pincher. This extreme may please the owners or board members, who would be making more money, but it would ultimately diminish customer satisfaction and employees' contentment.

So we find ourselves looking for the third option. In this case, balance would include a dash of spending and a pinch of frugality. We must learn to spend when the time calls for spending, but with careful consideration. Recognizing what is necessary spending or smart saving. The best way to accomplish this is to set realistic palpable goals. That way our attitude towards the politics of spending or not spending business money would cause all the ones involved to feel secure with our decisions.

Lack of business ethics vs. unrealistic ethics

In this area we could think that there is no such thing as too much ethics, but consider legal breaks that some of us may have a hard time using, simply for the fear of doing something we shouldn't. In Brazil they use the expression "Caxias" to refer to the person that would even compromise common sense in order to stick to the rules.

I can attest to that behavior because I acted like that for years. I realized that when someone bluntly told me to use my sick days to take off work when I was sick. I always felt guilty and pushed myself to make it into work, and for two years I wouldn't use my sick days. Somehow unrealistic expectations were brewing in my mind, and the behavior follows a pattern believing to be good ethics.

The opposite extreme normally uses the unrealistic side as an excuse to act unethically. This breeds from an initial lack of concern for morals in a personal level. Lack of ethics allows them to engage in practices that has as main focus personal gain at any cost. Just consider the business person who sees the bottom line as the only factor that matters, we can be sure that the well being of all involved is not even close to the top of the priorities list.

Our third option would be having knowledge of and respect for ethics involved in honest business. If we strive to see the bigger picture, we can, even a little selfishly, say that we are being honest for our own gain. The more honorable we are, the more trust we generate, with more trust comes more clients, better work from employees, and greater respect from competitors. When it comes to business ethics, we must start examining our own selves, and determine how honorable we must be in order gain respectable control, and not cheated or forceful control.

Chapter 7

Church

For many religious groups, and especially in today's America, the concept that politics are present within the church seems almost unscriptural. Realistically, in order to realize tasks and deal with different personalities who would like to accomplish their goals in hundreds of different ways, one must handle decisions with church politics in mind. No, we shouldn't water down the message, and no, the truth is not relative, but we are also able to present that same message, and achieve that same mission maintaining the amount of order necessary for a better final result.

For example: the church leadership could decide to change the order of service without conflicting with scripture, and still be a church that is doing exactly what the Bible wants us to do. They can approach this decision in two ways. First, they can simply do it because it is not wrong and they have the authority to do so. Or secondly, they can consider how that would affect different members, and eventually decide according to what would be best for the congregation.

Liberal vs. conservative

One prominent clash of extremes is the liberal versus conservative approach to church politics. Both sides can be so adamant about how they treat the subjects at hand. And frequently those extreme sides fail to consider the greater good and the needs to be fulfilled.

For instance, the liberal side wants changes, and what is working for the moment. The general perception is that the status quo is inherently bad. The approaches and techniques that have been done for years can no longer be effective. Therefore, we must fight for liberation from a decrepit system which is outdated and inefficient. This attitude certainly translates into a tactless and sometimes logically flawed approach towards church politics.

On the other side we find the conservative approach, which may sound satisfactory for some, but since we are dealing with extremes, this side also has its downfalls. Conservative politics tend to cling to the motto "it's better to err on the safe side." I'd like to point out that when it comes to church politics to err is to err. There is no safe side. To cling to certain positions simply for the sake of tradition can be just as dangerous as changing for the sake of change.

In the realm of church politics it is of the utmost importance to find the balance between these two sides. The third side of the coin would be able to adapt to the changes in culture and society, yet maintain important precepts that are timeless. Otherwise, we may find ourselves simply reacting to the opposite side instead of remaining balanced and doing things because they are right.

"Holier than thou" vs. "Everyone is ok"

This set of extremes is more abstract. It becomes more difficult to pinpoint when certain lines are crossed, because we would be dealing with people's intentions and attitudes. Nevertheless certain statements may make clear where one stands.

Let's start with someone's statement that gives the impression of an extreme view. "Church service is not for sinners!" I could hardly believe what I was hearing. As I kept listening, I came to understand the view, granted I still don't agree with it, but I can see the rational that lead to such thinking. It is a clear extreme, easily classified as an undesirable position. But reality shows that there are more people with such attitudes than we can imagine. A poor approach to church politics is the one which, in an unspoken way, declares "I am better than you, and that's why we'll do it my way!", "My spiritual life is in better shape than yours!" or "My sins are not as bad as yours, so we should listen to me!"

I know it sounds almost ridiculous when we point it out like this, but when you talk to people and they actually behave in certain ways, or say things that express that mindset, it is a sobering moment. We realize that this actually exists and people actually choose their actions based upon that mentality. You can see how such extreme begs to be fought against, and ends up generating the opposite reaction.

When people become appalled by such position, they tend to react by jumping to the other side of the fence, which encompasses the "everyone is ok" mentality. Whoever stated that "the voice of the people is the voice of God" was highly mistaken. It is dangerous to make decisions in church with a mindset that "everyone is ok". Many times the herd doesn't know when to cross the river, and much of the cattle could be lost if the cowboy let the herd decide for itself or let the young calf call the shots.

If everyone is ok, then what direction do we go? Consider this: Mom, dad, and three sons are on a road trip. Dad is at the wheel when they come to a junction with five possible paths. Each individual has an opinion of which road they must take. If everyone is right in their way, which road is the right road to their final destination? The paradox is similar when it comes to church politics and doctrinal issues. There is only one path. When we disagree, either I am wrong and you are right, or I am right and you are wrong, or both of us are wrong and someone else is right, but we cannot both be right.

When it comes to church politics a coin toss can end up in a proud boastful approach to what must be accomplished/ practiced or in a careless approach where anything goes as long as everyone is happy. The third side of the coin, which takes much effort to be maintained, would include an understanding attitude but yet firm knowledge of logical truths. Simply stated "we will take this route because the facts, documentation, evidence show that it will take us where we need to go." Yes, we must listen to each other and consider their feelings and opinions! Ultimately, a decision must be made without rejecting other possibilities simply because "we are better than they are."

"Calling privilege a right creates an undeserved sense of entitlement!"

Chapter 8

Government

This one is pretty obvious; politics are the center of all government dealings. The common person may get irritated by things we see on TV, news we hear about laws passed, and especially when tax time comes around. All those are necessary "evils" for our society to function properly. We may get fed up with some of the issues, but for any country to run its course, government politics are a must.

The intricacies of our economical system, tied to our social interactions, plus our educational and health system are so complex that little decisions made by one politician can shake the entire structure. Imagine a fruit tree loaded; then we grab its trunk and give it a good shake. If the fruits simply fall in the basket of another person standing by, everything is great. But if instead of falling in the basket, it falls on their heads, we may have some problems. The people in our nation are under the canopy of our government. The branches spread across different fields with politicians working to collect the fruits and keep an entire nation happy.

The recipe for extremes is set. We can, with no trouble, see how waffling on either side can have catastrophic results for someone's political career, or for the social group affected by such decisions. Therefore, we must strive to find the third side of the coin, enabling us to have a differing view on political issues and yet maintain order in our society.

Eternal Politician vs. Short term Politician

In the world of politics, a person must find their balance in the arena if they are to do the greater good to society and remain in power to keep doing so. But the reality is that some will fall "heads" on our first extreme. The eternal politician is usually using his expertise to keep him in office. It is not hard to understand this proposition and see some of their practices and consequences deriving from such behavior.

The eternal politician is so worried about remaining in office that he/she may not stand for certain positions, which should be fought for, simply because that may not get them re-elected. He/She knows how to work the system so that the work is being recognized and the dirt is swept under the rug. Succumbing to lobbyists to guarantee a future support or nomination can become a common practice of such individuals. Ultimately, the question that hangs in their minds is "Is this going to get me re-elected?"

The consequence of this extreme is a politician who is at the end of the day looking out for number one when he/she was actually elected to look out for others. Compromises which may affect society in a damaging way may take place in backroom deals. I am not talking about illegal things; after all, they want to remain in office. I am talking about completely legal things that do not have the best interests of the people at heart. The eternal politician forgets the purpose of such office, and instead of serving the people, he/she uses the political machine to serve self.

One might think that with a picture painted like that, the opposite is definitely the right answer. Flip the coin to the other side and we will find the short-term politician. This type will shake the foundations of any level of government. This politician will stand strong on his/her principles, and move towards bold policies and issues. It sounds appealing, but in reality it is not ideal either.

The short-term politician may bring about much good in a short time, but one must realize that a nation doesn't cease to exist in one term. The work of a politician must take in consideration the now, the near future, and the distant future. The general behavior of a short-term politician may burn bridges that will eventually keep them from being re-elected or that will generate animosity with those who could solidify a greater good for the future.

Allow me to illustrate a situation in which thinking short-term may be detrimental. We all agree that education is an important area when it comes to politics. We would probably agree when a politician makes a case for new equipment in our school district; in fact, his inspirational speech would move us to demand those improvements. Looking from the ground level, Mr. Short-term is a saint. We may have missed is the fact that the same people that Mr. Short-term is burning bridges with today are the ones who were going to (but not anymore!) support him two years from now when the scheduled discussion on teachers' salaries would come to a vote. Is the improvement for now good? Yes, but if we weigh on a scale what would have brought better results in our children's education, we may find that we have missed the boat.

Once again we must find the third side. In this case, it's a Politician who is able to remain in office without compromising his/her values, but knows when to strike or retreat so that the greater good is accomplished. The key to this situation is when the politician can manage to do things for the good of the people without burning bridges and yet have enough to show so that he/she may be able to remain in office. If this coin is going to remain spinning, the politician must never forget why he/she is in office. I understand that what we have here is basically a utopian concept, and we can be highly discouraged by the political world, but as stated before, remaining balanced on the third side of the coin is not an easy task; it takes effort that so many are not willing to put forth.

Liberal vs. conservative

In our political world, the eternal battle between liberal and conservative is the epitome of popular disenchantment with our government. People perceive that the government no longer has their best interest in mind. During election months these two sides come to a full-out clash and as they point fingers at each other, we sample a distinct preview of both extremes.

The liberal side battles wholeheartedly to convince us that big government is the way to go. Government must step in and do for us what we will not do for ourselves. Social equality must be enforced at all costs. The interesting techniques used to present those ideals have long created a sense of distrust in the general public. We must also consider the consequences of leaning towards this extreme. It seems like a far cry but the decay of the capitalist system could become a reality.

Consider this: if you make more money because you worked your way up through the ranks, the sense of accomplishment together with the physical rewards motivate you to work better. If we take that away by pressing the idea that if you make more you will pay more, we therefore forfeit the motivating factor causing a general lack of stimulus to work better. It should be easy to spot how an extreme approach on this side of the coin can be detrimental to our society.

For our conservative fellow countrymen, we must also indicate that the opposite extreme isn't that pleasant either. Certain changes must take place as we adapt to the needs of an ever-evolving society. If one is stuck to a conservative position simply because it has worked in the past, it can be a precarious position to maintain.

Take for instance our fuel situation. The country is constantly fearful of where the next turn may take us. Changes in gas prices are nothing new, but the feeling of uncertainty makes the public weary. An extreme approach to this situation would say "oil has moved this country for the past so many years, so why should we mess with a good thing?" Add to it the oil industry lobbyists who love this "conservative" approach to politics in this area, and we have the right mixture to keep this country back in the 20th century. If we know that there are alternative sources of energy, what is keeping us from investing our efforts into it?

A balanced approach would count the cost, measure the changes in times, adapt when necessary and remain firm on unchangeable truths. Some things that may have destroyed empires in the past may destroy us today, or some things that may have slowed down progress in the past may be keeping us from turning a new chapter in our world today. Change for the sake of change (i.e. liberals) is dangerous and irresponsible, and stubbornness (i.e. conservatives) for the sake of pride and power is humanistic and foolish. It is to the best interest of society that our politicians most certainly need to embrace an agenda that has, in fact, the greater good of the country in mind.

Section II
Quick Review

In politics, the third side of the coin would facilitate a harmonious environment in every area of our lives. If we keep the coin spinning creating that third side, we enable ourselves to maintain a wise perspective of our decisions whether:

- we are still in school,
- we are grown ups in the real world,
- it affects us in church,
- it affects our political views.

If we are balanced in this area we would be able to influence the outcome of many political endeavors in various arenas of our lives.

Section III

"Knowledge without action is like seeing a wall and not stepping on the brake!"

Personal Choices

Our personal lives are filled with sides, choices, extremes. Our personal issues, our fears, our day-to-day choices all can be approached with a "Heads or Tails" mentality when in reality we should be approaching those personal factors with a well-balanced point of view.

How we treat each other and handle ourselves, how we face our fears, how we entertain ourselves, and how much we choose to be absorbed by any of those choices are all factors determining future outcomes.

Personal choices involve all the little details of our life. We must choose if we will go to work happy or be a grumpy co-worker to those around us. We must consider sticking to our choices or accepting suggestions. We need to consciously determine our reaction to little incidents that will happen throughout our day.

Falling on one side or the other could be an extreme that brings us more headaches than we would be willing to handle. Therefore, if the first personal choice we can make is the one to avoid extremes and look into a balanced third option, then we will be able to move towards our daily affairs and analyze our choices with a favorable disposition.

Since we are held accountable primarily for the choices we make and actions we take, one must give careful consideration to all those trivial selections that could potentially alter the course of our day, or even our lives. Areas such as personal issues, entertainment, and ethics certainly shape the path that is ahead of us.

Chapter 9

Personal Issues

Many psychologists will agree with me when I say that we all need therapy. We are a people filled with issues. A great number of Americans have issues that have been diagnosed. The truth is we all have issues, but since they don't affect our ordinary interactions, we don't feel the need to address them.

The problem is the fact that our issues do affect our interactions, but we are so set in the mentality that "this is just who I am" that we don't realize that this "ME" is actually stuck in one side of the coin.

Over reacting vs. under reacting

The over reacting side can be compared to the junior high love. Everything is so accentuated by "No one knows how it feels", "It's the end of the world if she breaks up with me", or "Nobody understands me" statements. If we choose not to be politically correct and protect the "self-esteem" of that child, we would bluntly call those "drama queens". This is the person who treats every challenge, every slip on the smooth flow of things as a major catastrophe.

We can be patient and bear with such individuals, but the danger starts when situations that could be easily controlled become a big ordeal. Or when groups must work together and the over-reacting person cannot be approached for fear of huge emotional explosions. Such behavior impairs all lines of communication, leaving no room for reason, patience or good measure.

There is a clear distinction between a single event when someone overreacts and a pattern of behavior. We all know the guy in office, or the girl in school, or the lady in church, or the neighbor man who we all hesitate to approach with a comment or suggestion, whom we dread if we find ourselves having to work with them. So I believe it is clear that we are not talking about those who have a bad day, and we just happened to be the unlucky "straw that broke the camel's back."

Some people make the mistake of deciding to react so that those explosions never occur. They populate the under reacting group. The opposite extreme is less damaging to the group and more damaging to oneself, therefore we tend to overlook them since their behavior only affects us if we depend on their decisions.

Some of the characteristics of the under reacting person include "no sugar, no salt" personality, uncaring behavior (If it doesn't directly affect me, I don't care about it), freezing under pressure (I must react, but I don't want to, so I freeze), and/or "not a go-getter" personality. Either by choice or by psychological incapacitation, the under reacting person will do whatever it takes not to raise an upheaval. The basic train of thought is if I don't react I don't have to deal with it.

Some of you are probably bouncing on your seats, just by picturing someone actually behaving like such around you. But we don't need to overreact to the under reactors' reaction. There is a third option which we must choose to react appropriately according to each individual situation. There is a time to be angry and scream, there is a time to do nothing, and there is also a time to calmly address the situation in front of us knowing that it is not the end of the world, that "I can do what I can, and beyond that it is out of my hands." This would be a balanced reaction.

Excessive determination vs. apathy

You probably noticed how excessive determination and apathy can be present in many areas of our lives. We can assume that the root of such behavior is within ourselves, our personal issues. Somehow, somewhere or someone has planted the seed for a personal issue to develop in our minds. Maybe the constant attempts as a child to get your father's approval have created a pattern of behavior that overflows into other areas of your life.

If we add certain behaviors embedded in us by our family micro-cosmos to the greater societal influence of immediate gratification, we find ourselves knee-deep in a mentality that says "I want what I want and I want it now." As a person starts acting upon such mentality, the natural progression of things would lead us to believe that this individual develops an inability to perceive the bigger picture. Long term effects of actions taken hastily are no longer considered, when all we are interested in is what I can get from it right now.

Allow me to share with you a few examples that might shine a light on this side of the coin. Have you ever encountered a couple determined to get married, in spite of all the red flags and advice of their friends and family? Their determination blinds them to what is so obvious to everyone else. Or a business person who is so determined to succeed that his/her family is neglected. Maybe the college student who is highly determined to get the best grades that they forget to have fun, and vice-versa. There are many scenarios where excessive determination has taken a healthy drive to excel and transformed it into a personal choice that can hurt not only the individual but also many loved ones.

But the other side of the coin doesn't look so bright either. It is not healthy to go through life with a "Whatever you say is fine" attitude. Just as in all the other areas of our life, apathy can be a highly damaging attitude to have. As you can easily see, apathy could affect relationships, career choices, and day-to-day interactions. It all starts with a personal decision to care or not to care about something.

Picture the person who is not affected by an emergency at work or the person who would not be fazed by a child getting injured. Maybe imagine the guy who is not emotionally moved in any direction when dumped by his girlfriend. That should paint a clear image of apathy. If I simply don't react to something, things will be ok, and if I leave it alone long enough, someone will take care of it.

It is hard to believe that people aim to become excessively determined or apathetic. These are extremes that we slip into slowly through every little choice we make. Since it is our choices, then I would suggest that we make choices which will keep us balanced.

We must create for ourselves an attitude which allows us to move towards a goal and not lose perspective of the bigger picture. Also, we must decide to deal with issues or situations that may paralyze us in a non-apathetic way. Leave the running and hiding under the bed until the problem goes away to the children. Each individual must find his/her own limits when it comes to excessive determination and apathy.

Eat too much vs. eat too little

This set of personal issues will not only affect our psychological health, but will also have a direct effect on our physical health. As a person chooses to dive into one extreme or the other, he/she embarks on a journey that so many find themselves trapped into. Our choices when it comes to our eating habits can determine our future just as much as other personal choices we make in life. One side sees food as a friend, a way of escape, and the other side perceives food as the enemy, the cause of his/her problems.

If we were to deal with this choice with the toss of a coin, we would find ourselves in a precarious position. If it falls "heads" we will turn to eating too much for comfort, or if it falls "tails," we will blame food for our problems and eat too little to become someone else. The first side generally causes us to focus on obesity. If we average the information of different sources, we find out that approximately 3.8 million Americans are over 300lbs. Therefore, it is easy to jump to the conclusion that this is the only problem associated with eating too much.

That was not the case with Mr. Doe. He was not an obese person, maybe not as fit as he could be, but not showing any signs of real weight problems. Mr. Doe had spent portions of his childhood wondering if there would be food on the table for the next meal. He had grown up in a poor family. As he worked his way out of poverty, he vowed to never have to worry about not having enough food in his fridge. And so he did have and he did eat what he wanted, whenever he wanted. In his mid-forty's Mr. Doe had a heart attack and didn't make it. When the doctors examined him they informed his family that because of the way he ate, even if they brought him in three months earlier it would still have been too late.

The flip side is a touchy one, because it is virtually impossible to approach someone about their little food intake without hurting some feelings and creating a certain friction. But we must not neglect the fact that about 11 million Americans fight this battle everyday. The only one who can help is the one suffering from this disorder. We know that until we decide for ourselves to do something about it, to ask for help, no one can make us deal with it. Usually this type of personal issue starts with a distorted self image, which will eventually escalate to unhealthy levels.

It is not hard to find information, articles, or images on this subject. Many television shows have shed light on this self-destructive behavior. We have become very aware that it is a problem, but the challenge lies in the fact that many people stuck on this side of the coin remain in denial, thinking that "I'm not like that", "I don't really have a problem". This is an extreme that can only be dealt with when we stop lying to ourselves and admit that this may be our case, and we do need help.

The third side in this case is fairly simple, not easy, but simple. We must create a realistic perception that food is simply fuel for us to keep living our lives. Just like an automobile, if you take the fuel away it will die, but if you dump too much fuel in the carburetor it will choke. We must eat what our bodies need when our bodies need it; and if we find ourselves looking for food or avoiding food because of emotional issues, then we must stop ourselves or search for help before it becomes an extreme that could cost our life.

"Tudo que e' demais, sobra!"

Tia Dolores

Chapter 10

Entertainment/Recreation

Entertainment has been around for a long time. Painting, music, and theater have been around for thousands of years fulfilling the artistic needs of man. Games were invented probably to quench the thirst of our competitive side. And activities to pass time were most likely created the first time man found himself trapped in a situation where time was abundant. It is interesting that we can find extremes even in the way we entertain ourselves.

We have the ability to take something that was created to help us keep our sanity in a stressful world and transform it into an obsession, or kill it under false assumptions. There are so many activities we engage in as hobbies and all of them have therapeutic effects in our psyche, but just as easily as any other area in our lives, we can flip that coin and land heads or tails. In modern time, recreation such as television, sports and hobbies have occupied much of the non-working hours of the common family.

If we invest so many hours in such activities, and if these hours focus on one extreme or the other, we are defeating the true purpose of entertainment which is to give people pleasure and relaxation.

Television:
The evil destroying families vs.
the magical box keeping parents' sanity

No other way of entertainment has defined society, or shaped our minds to the magnitude reached by the television. An invention that reached its full form in the early 1900s has changed the face of the 20th century. Something carrying so much influential power can effortlessly instigate extreme approaches to its use. Just as stated before, it is possible to have too much of a good thing.

The extreme that excludes television from our lives would argue that it is destroying our families. Some of the arguments are valid but let's not "throw away the baby with the bath water." This side would blame the television for everything bad that our kids learn. The reality that the amount of time we spend as a society in front of the tube is in fact detrimental to families doesn't justify a witch hunt.

How much is television actually to blame for certain behaviors? Heads would affirm that all of the blame lies with the television. This side could focus on the wrong things being taught on TV shows or the indecency portrayed as an acceptable standard. If this position had enough power to convince society, we would most likely be sold on the idea that we must get rid of our TV sets in order to fix all of society's problems.

Tails, on the other hand, wouldn't know what to do with their lives if the television disappeared. For those on the opposite side, TV sets are what keeps them sane. It is the cheapest babysitter a parent can find. What parent hasn't at one point or another hoped for a way to quiet their little ones down? When that button is pressed and the high-pitched buzzing sound announces that cartoons are on, the kids stop what they are doing and are captured by the colors, images and sounds coming out of that box. That is a magical moment that some parents may come to over-utilize.

The consequences of such a parental mistake affect children in a frightening way. To rely on strangers to

99

determine what our children are exposed to is a blunder that many parents may come to regret. It is true that television is not the source of all evil, but it is also true that TV is not a magical box either.

The third side of the coin would have TV as a tool. Think of a hammer and how it can be harmful, useful, or useless. If we hit the nail on the head, the hammer is useful. If we hit our finger, it is harmful. And if we miss it completely, it is useless. It is all a matter of how we use it. So it is the television. We can use it as an educational tool that could assist us with our children. It can entertain us and give a small escape from reality relieving some stress. The secret lies in our control of it. We determine what our children watch and how much of it. We determine what and how much we watch. The choice is ours to make. The TV is an inanimate object that is as good or as bad as we make it to be.

Sports:
Complete repugnance of athletes' abilities vs. idolizing a human being

Our society is flooded with all sorts of sports that we can watch or play. The number-one pastime in America is a sport. It can be simply for entertainment purposes as we watch it or for recreational purposes as we play with our family and friends. This is another category of entertainment that can generate a coin toss, a possibility of developing one extreme or another.

As we shine the spotlight on great athletes, some individuals have demonstrated a certain repugnance to such characters. Here are some views of such a position. First they would argue that there is no value to their skill. As talented as they are, their skill contributes in no way, shape, or form to the improvement of society. Second, they may state that the intrinsic value of their trait is for entertainment purposes only. And finally, they would have a strong case when pointing out character flaws and attitudes that are a denigrating influence.

Certainly the fight would be on if heads were to face tails in a debate about the value of sports in our lives. The opposite side could point out how these athletes are the peak of what a man should be (physically speaking). Maybe they would try to dispute that they deserve every dime they make. They have worked through the years to throw, kick, bat, hit, or shoot a ball with such precision that we are privileged to watch such a display of excellence.

The extreme gets worse when a passion for a player leads this side to overlook their brushes with the law. When we find ourselves justifying what an athlete may have done, we are indirectly declaring that they are above the law. Sometimes we plainly don't want to believe they are guilty because in our minds they can do no wrong; they are perfect role models. That is an extreme that blinds us with our own infatuation with an icon created by our entertainment industry.

When it comes to sports as a way of entertainment, we can keep ourselves balanced by giving honor to whom honor is due. It is possible to admire a person's ability and not idolize them. It is possible to keep our jealousy of someone's accomplishments under control. I can be entertained by watching a sport of my preference and maintain my real perception of the athletes in check. I know they are not perfect but they are great at what they do. I also know they get paid an absurd amount, but if I was in their place I wouldn't be complaining. All we can do is take the inspiring stories, the work ethics, and the examples of the ones who are great role models and make good use of what they have to offer.

Hobbies:
Time consuming vs. Non-existent

Some describe hobbies as fulfilling a desire outside our main job. We may never pursue a career in the music industry, but some of us still pick that guitar when alone at home. We may not be the next Van Gough, but some enjoy spending hours in front of the canvas every time we get a chance. Others may glue their eyes to a video game, or glue the pieces of a miniature model together. The majority of us have them. Hobbies can be a great source of stress relief. But we are not studying the self controlled, well balanced behavior, so we turn our attention to how even something as inoffensive as a hobby can be taken to an extreme.

The first side is the "no hobbies" person. If someone chooses not to have a hobby period, it is an extreme. How can we make such a statement? Considering that a hobby is any activity used for us to enjoy our free time, if someone doesn't engage in any of such activities, he/she has forfeited any escape valve for self expression and/or stress relief. It would be an indicator that the individual isn't dedicating any time to take care of self.

The people on this side of the coin tend to be workaholics, melancholics, or excessively determined to accomplish certain things in life. They don't have time for a hobby because that would take time away from what they are focused on at this moment. This individual ignores some of the basic needs of our emotional health. Even those who are lucky enough to find their dream job, and basically have one of their hobbies as their way of making a living, have certain activities apart

103

from their work for when they need a break from all the responsibilities. So the absence of a hobby can be categorized as an extreme.

The other extreme surges when someone becomes obsessed with their hobby. We must remember that a hobby is supposed to assist us in maintaining a healthy lifestyle. When a hobby takes over our lives we tend to spend so much money on it, and it eventually takes more and more time away from our families and the other interactions of our lives. When we lose sight of the purpose of such hobbies, we could put them on the top of a priorities list and neglect areas that shouldn't be ignored.

How would you like to be on the receiving end of such behavior? A parent, or spouse, maybe even a friend who has become highly involved with a hobby, starts to neglect his responsibilities. This month's budget may be tight but he must have what he needs for the hobby. The kids are failing math, but she doesn't have the time to help, "I'm not even that good in math." The excuses start flowing. All the friends have become distant. "They don't understand," he says to justify such behavior. It sounds extreme, but you would be surprised by how many people fall into such trap.

Once again we find ourselves looking for a third option. Since it is healthy to have a hobby, we cannot simply throw it out the window for fear of a possible obsession. Here is how we can be balanced about our hobbies. We must set limits for ourselves. Those must be thought through before we get highly involved; otherwise they may not be realistic. We must decide how much time is too much time, and how much money is too much money.

We must always remember that a hobby is always secondary to our family and work. If we find ourselves dreading our time with our family because it is taking our time away from our hobby, then we may need to back away from that hobby for a while. If our budget is getting strained because our passion for an activity is determining how much we spend and not our bank account, maybe it is time to focus on something else for a while. Keeping ourselves in check is the best way to keep a hobby in its place.

"Real change is only
possible when it takes place
within us!"

Chapter 11

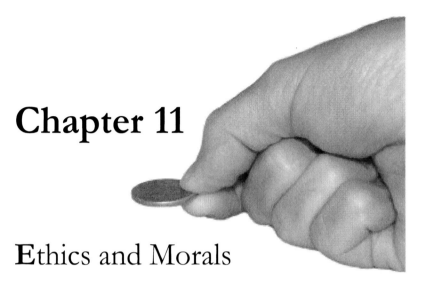

Ethics and Morals

My wife made an interesting statement, or better yet, a profound question that cuts deep into the heart of this chapter. As we drove out of our driveway she said, "What keeps someone from stealing our mail?" Think about it! It is just sitting there, neither lock nor any special security system. For that matter, what keeps us from doing what is wrong when no one is looking? Some may say the law. But what keeps the upstanding citizens from doing something they shouldn't even if they would never get caught?

There is a boundary inside each one of us called morals or ethics. How those are developed is still a highly debatable subject. Different people may carry a different set of standards, but the truth is that ethics and morals maintain society's equilibrium. Without a certain sense of right and wrong, or without a certain code which instills in us the desire to do what is right simply because it is right, businesses would be fraudulent, parents would have no grounds to punish their children, immorality would be as subjective as a dice roll.

This group of spoken and unspoken code of ethics keeps us at work, keeps a doctor from performing certain procedures, keeps a child safe from predators, and keeps us doing the best we can with the cards life deals us.

At Work: Workaholic vs. laziness

Work ethic entitles a full picture of our attitude towards our jobs or the way we do our jobs. The two most extreme and with the most side effects are the workaholic and the lazy worker. Both are very harmful to self, family and society. Therefore, we must search for a strong middle ground where we can stand in balance. In that search for the third side of the coin, we need to investigate these two extremes.

Some may see it as a dedicated worker when someone spends countless hours at work. If working 90 hours a week was healthy, there would be no need for workers' rights. The reason we have laws regarding

108

how many hours we can work without a break and similar rules is because someone found out that we need those breaks, and that we need that recovery time before we can get back to work. Some major victims of such behavior are the families of those displaying such behavior. Ultimately, workaholism will make our work more inefficient. Anyone with a workaholic parent can attest to the pain that this extreme can cause.

On the flip side, we find the ones who know all the loopholes to get out of work and still get the paycheck, or maybe how to stretch a job to last twice the time that it actually takes. The lazy worker knows how to do only what is necessary. His/her lack of decent work ethic makes it easy to focus on number one, and nothing else. Never applying oneself because there is no physical reward. This person will do the minimum to keep his/her job.

This type of behavior is usually easily spotted and that pushes that individual into the job-hopping pattern. You get hired, then the boss notices your true work ethic, and soon you are looking for another job. If a boss doesn't notice the lazy attitude because you have mastered your schemes, then most likely your co-workers would start feeling the burden that you put on them, and in the best case scenario you keep a job where people are annoyed by your work ethic.

The ideal position to stand on would most likely be one that keeps you motivated at work. As far as you know, you will do the best you can; but when it is time to go home, you should be able to drop the pen, turn off the computer, or put down the telephone and go home. The measure of a good worker should not be how many more hours he/she worked, but how well he/she utilized those hours. Good work ethics would tell us to work well when our bosses are watching and just as well when they are not. It would also tell us to not let work make us neglect ourselves, family, and friends.

At Home:
Morality ignored because of over teaching vs. morality unknown because of lack of teaching

I am a strong believer that the morality line that is so debated is actually created at home. Our upbringing has a major influence on our perception of morality. In this case the ones affected by our ethics are our little ones. Our actions or lack of can shape our children's worldview. As a kid, I remember how hypocritical I thought my mother was when she would smack my mouth for using bad words, and the very next sentence out of her mouth were dripping with such words. She didn't realize that her example was teaching me more than her rebuke. The two sides of this coin are only one of many ethical questions when it comes to family and children's upbringing.

Many parents are eager to make sure their child is learning the proper way to behave, or what is right and wrong. Some are over-protective making sure they do not expose them to any bad example. These parents are constantly "teaching" their kids. There are teachable moments when we can use certain circumstances to impart a sense of morality, but if a parent doesn't learn when enough is enough, this extreme could accentuate the rebellious years. After a while, over-teaching numbs the child to our teaching and starts working against us.

But we should not jump to the other side. We must be careful not to overlook those teachable moments. We also should not assume that morality will be taught in the schools. Teachers may do the best they can, but the responsibility lies with the parents. Some of us are afraid of pushing our children too hard, so we choose to "err on the side of caution", but it is a flawed reaction to our fear that our little ones "won't like us".

Have you ever wondered why a parent won't discipline their kids when it is obviously necessary? Either they don't know how to, or they are afraid of their children's reaction. Discipline is a direct way to impress morality in a kid's life. This is an area in life which may take generations to fix once the morality line is corrupted. The impact is difficult to quantify and by the time it becomes obvious enough to be perceived, the damage is already done, and it is a long road to recovery.

This is a third side that many of us hesitate saying anything about, because parents tend to be very defensive about how they raise their kids. But when it comes to morality and how we pass it down to our kids, balance must be achieved if we are going to be successful in maintaining moral standards. Imagine a world without ethical or moral limits, without that invisible barrier that keeps us from just doing as we please. We must strive to find our individual balance in how we teach our children. We can respect how parents don't want to be told how to raise their kids, so this side of the coin will require a decent amount of self monitoring.

In Society: Prude vs. immoral

We live in a society where all our freedoms have allowed certain behaviors to be legally acceptable, but personally individuals frown upon such behaviors. It is not feasible to try to legislate morality, so we must draw those lines on a personal level. If we get stuck on one side or the other, we may compromise a healthy lifestyle. A person can be described as being overly concerned with decorum or propriety, a prude person. Or on the opposite side, we could find an immoral person, someone who has a disregard for that code of conduct held to be authoritative in matters of right and wrong.

On one side of the coin we deal with the position where a person is oblivious to normal interactions; that happens due to a prudish approach to morality. This extreme perceives the simple fact of being aware of certain immoral behaviors as wrong. The prude has chosen to isolate him/herself from society. Maybe this isolation doesn't happen physically but psychologically. A way to measure if we have reached a point that is in fact detrimental is to look at how our perception of morality damages our healthy interactions.

An interesting example is the classic parent-child interaction. If a parent reaches the prudish extreme, he can become oblivious to the challenges, influences, and immoral behaviors that may be present in the child's life. Therefore if a parent is unaware of such behavior, he won't seize the opportunity to impede, correct or discipline such behaviors. A major disconnection may occur between parent and child.

Some may look at the prude and decide that the opposite side is the way to go. Immorality is an extreme that may seem pleasant at first. Who would not like the idea of doing whatever brings us pleasure whenever we feel like it? But the reality is that immoral behavior is ultimately damaging in the long run. It can affect our work, our health, and our relationships.

Let's try this scenario. Promiscuous dating choices may seem fun and adventurous for some, but besides the health risks that are automatically attached to such, we also deal with psychological side effects. If a person develops a sense of commitment through an immoral lifestyle, he/she will find it difficult to settle down at a time when that is desired. Chances are that such a lifestyle would most likely attract other people who also have a certain standard of morality which is not conducive to healthy relationships.

There are many other consequences to falling on one side or the other of this morality coin. The third option would require an awareness of immoral behavior but not necessarily an approval of such. We can be informed of life choices that are present in our world even if we recognize it as immoral. A balanced position would choose to avoid immorality and yet not fit the prude profile. I believe purity is the key word. When we think of precious metals, we associate purity with its

114

value. The more pure the metal, the more we pay for it. If our moral standard is without these flaws (lack of awareness or the blemish of immorality), then we have a valuable asset within ourselves.

As a boss looking to hire someone, who would you prefer as a future candidate? A person who is a prude, a person who is immoral, or a person who is highly moral with a smartly aware worldview? The purity in our ethical or moral standards will develop healthy behaviors in every area of our lives. We can choose not to drink and drive because it is the right thing to do, and not because we could get caught. We can choose the right behavior because it is the best choice for the greater good even if what we want right now seems more desirable. The balanced side is the most efficient option if we desire to live profitable lives to ourselves, others, and society.

Section III
Quick Review

Our issues shape the choices in our lives. We must deal with our psychological issues so that we can maintain our healthy interactions and functions on a daily basis. We must choose how to entertain ourselves without crossing lines which would defeat the purpose of such entertainment. All of those choices can be affected by our set of morals, our ethical vein. Finding the third side of the personal choices coin can lead us to a highly profitable lifestyle.

The Next Step...

We reached the end of this journey. The search for third sides continues as we look to apply this concept to all other areas of our lives. The possibilities are endless. We can apply the "neither heads nor tails" ideology to religion, to businesses, to neighborhood dealings, and so on. Name a situation and try for yourself to find the extremes where people can take such a situation, and then establish the balanced third option.

Relationships, politics, and personal choices are just a great example of how all areas of our lives are interconnected and how dangerous it could be to become stuck on one side of the coin. We must always strive to remain spinning, looking at both sides to make decisions that have considered heads and tails, and have found the answer which better suits each independent situation.

It is possible for us to ruin our lives with too much of a good thing, so we must strive to have just the right amount. The coin has been tossed. It is up to us to make those calls, to decide if we will be the ones stuck on one side, or the ones who defy the norm and remain balanced without ever getting trapped in one extreme or the other. It's your call. Heads? Tails? Or neither?

Disclaimer

The materials consulted for this work were cited as faithfully as possible according to the APA style. All the stand-alone quotes are the original work of the author. It is this work's intent to be no more than an opinion essay that may encourage the readers to develop an open mind when dealing with average day-to-day decisions. The views expressed here are a simple reflection of the conclusions derived from many of the author's personal experiences, and as such no part of this work should be taken out of context, nor should this theory be utilized to form creeds or systems of belief. If the thoughts in this book bring to light personal issues more serious than our everyday headaches, do not use this work as a means to find healing. Be sure to seek qualified professional help!

References

Cambridge advanced learner's dictionary (3rd ed.). (2008). : Cambridge University press.

Kim, B. (2007). Why drinking too much water is dangerous. Retrieved March 23, 2008, from http://www.drbenkim.com

Martin, G. (n.d.). The Phrase Finder. Retrieved March 23, 2008, from http://www.phrases.org.uk/meanings/387400.html

Overbearing. (2000). In American heritage dictionary. Retrieved March 23, 2008, from http://www.bartleby.com/61/66/O0176600.html

Rosenthal, N. E. (1998). Winter Blues: Seasonal affective disorder - what it is and how to overcome it (Revised ed.). New York, NY: The Guilford Press.

Singer, B. W. (2000, March 26). Raising a perfect child. Boston Globe Magazine, ¶ 18-20.

Wooltorton, E. (2003, July 8). Too much of a good thing? Toxic effects of vitamin and mineral supplements. Canadian Medical Association Journal, 169(1), Table 1. Retrieved March 23, 2008, from www.cmaj.ca/cgi/content-nw/full/169/1/47/T127